LIFE DURING
WORLD WAR II

by Wendy H. Lanier

Content Consultant
Travis Hardy, PhD
Department of History
University of Tennessee

Core Library

An Imprint of Abdo Publishing
www.abdopublishing.com

www.abdopublishing.com

Published by Abdo Publishing, a division of ABDO, PO Box 398166, Minneapolis, Minnesota 55439. Copyright © 2015 by Abdo Consulting Group, Inc. International copyrights reserved in all countries. No part of this book may be reproduced in any form without written permission from the publisher. Core Library™ is a trademark and logo of Abdo Publishing.

Printed in the United States of America, North Mankato, Minnesota
092014
012015

THIS BOOK CONTAINS
RECYCLED MATERIALS

Cover Photo: AP Images
Interior Photos: AP Images, 1, 4, 7, 12, 18, 20, 22, 38, 45; US Navy, 9; Red Line Editorial, 16; Office of Price Administration, 25; Everett Collection/Newscom, 28, 34; Bettmann/Corbis, 30; The Mariners' Museum/Corbis, 32; Dan Grossi/AP Images, 36; Tom Fitzsimmons/AP Images, 40; Mirrorpix/Newscom, 42

Editor: Mirella Miller
Series Designer: Becky Daum

Library of Congress Control Number: 2014944230

Cataloging-in-Publication Data
Lanier, Wendy H.
 Life during World War II / Wendy H. Lanier.
  p. cm. -- (Daily life in US history)
 ISBN 978-1-62403-629-3 (lib. bdg.)
 Includes bibliographical references and index.
 1. World War--1939-1945--Juvenile literature.   2. World War--1939-1945--Social aspects--Juvenile literature.   I. Title.
 940.53--dc23
                                                    2014944230

CHAPTER ONE

THE UNITED STATES GOES TO WAR

The United States in the late 1930s was a gloomy place for many families. A poor economy meant many people were out of work. Most people were barely making enough money to survive. Many Americans were not paying attention to what was happening in other parts of the world.

A long line of jobless men waits for food in New York City during the Great Depression of the 1930s.

Start of World War II

Halfway around the world, the tiny nation of Japan was overpopulated. The country had limited resources. Japan was prepared to take more land and increase its resources using force. The Empire of Japan invaded its neighbor China in 1937.

At about the same time in Europe, German dictator Adolf Hitler took over Austria and Czechoslovakia. Then in 1939, Hitler and his troops invaded Poland. War broke out across Europe. Soon Japan joined forces with Germany, Italy, and four other countries to form the Axis Powers. Their goal was to take over the world. The world was at war for the second time in the 1900s.

Most people in the United States did not want to be part of another war. World War I (1914–1918) had taken many US lives. Americans did not want more lives to be lost defending other countries that seemed so far away. However, everything changed when the war came to the United States.

A small rescue boat searches for survivors after the USS West Virginia was bombed at Pearl Harbor.

Wake-Up Call

Sunday, December 7, 1941, started out much like any other day. The war in Europe and Asia seemed far away. Americans went about their business as usual.

A Game Changer

Before the attack on Pearl Harbor, the US government supported the Allied forces. The Allies included the United Kingdom, France, the Soviet Union, China, Poland, the Netherlands, and approximately 12 other countries. The United States hoped the Allies would win the war. The US government sent weapons and supplies, but they did not send US soldiers. After the attack on Pearl Harbor, the mood of the country changed overnight. At first people were shocked. Then they became angry. Within a few hours of the events at Pearl Harbor, most Americans were ready to join the fight.

Shortly after noon in Bogalusa, Louisiana, ten-year-old Billy Hinote and his sister, Bernice, were returning home from church. Bounding into the living room, Billy came to a stop. Something was wrong. Billy's mother and father were listening to the radio with worried expressions on their faces. The radio report explained how Japanese forces had attacked Pearl Harbor. The Japanese had chosen to react to sanctions the US government had placed on Japan.

Much of the US Navy fleet was anchored at Pearl Harbor in 1941.

Pearl Harbor was a US naval base on the island of Oahu, Hawaii. Many US soldiers were housed on nearby army bases. Army and navy airplanes were parked on nearby airfields. The attack on Pearl Harbor was a major setback to US forces.

The scene in the Hinote home was replayed in almost every home in the United States. People heard

Doris "Dorie" Miller

The soldiers stationed at Pearl Harbor had no warning of the Japanese attack. The first wave of bombs occurred at 7:55 a.m. Twenty-two-year-old Doris "Dorie" Miller from Waco, Texas, was stationed at Pearl Harbor. He was serving aboard the USS *West Virginia*. At the sound of the alarm, Miller rushed to his assigned station. It was heavily damaged. Miller immediately reported above deck to help move the wounded to safety. He also manned a machine gun until he ran out of ammunition. For his bravery on that day, Miller was the first African American to be awarded the Navy Cross. The Navy Cross is the second highest military award for bravery in combat.

about the Pearl Harbor bombing on the radio or from a neighbor. The news came as a shock. But as the day wore on, Americans' anger grew. Americans were determined the Japanese would pay for what they had done.

After the attacks on Pearl Harbor, President Franklin Delano Roosevelt addressed Congress. He discussed how the events had changed Americans' attitudes. Then he asked Congress to declare war against the Empire of Japan:

> *The facts of yesterday and today speak for themselves. The people of the United States have already formed their opinions and well understand the implications to the very life and safety of our nation.*
>
> . . .
>
> *I ask that the Congress declare that since the unprovoked and dastardly attack by Japan on Sunday, December 7th, 1941, a state of war has existed between the United States and the Japanese empire.*
>
> Source: "Pearl Harbor Address to the Nation." American Rhetoric. American Rhetoric, Dec. 8, 1941. Web. Accessed July 28, 2014.

What's the Big Idea?

Take a close look at Roosevelt's speech. What is Roosevelt's main point about Pearl Harbor and the declaration of war on Japan? What can you tell about the American people's attitude after the attacks?

CHAPTER TWO

BACK TO WORK

Even before the attack on Pearl Harbor, the United States had been sending war materials to support the Allies. Factories were built or reopened from World War I. The factories made airplanes, tanks, warships, trucks, and weapons. The demand for these war supplies created many new jobs.

In 1941 fewer than 500,000 Americans were serving in the armed forces. After Pearl Harbor, tens

Men arrive at the US Army headquarters on December 8, 1941, to enlist and join the war effort.

The United States Goes Back to Work

During the Great Depression (late 1920s to mid-1940s), the rate of people without jobs reached approximately 23.6 percent. The economy was at an all-time low during the Great Depression. People were not spending money because they had very little. After the start of World War II, the demand for war materials created jobs. The nation's unemployment rate had fallen to 1.2 percent by 1944. It was the lowest in US history.

of thousands of American men joined the military service. By 1945 that number had risen to more than 16 million. With so many men serving in the nation's armed forces, the factories had no workers. Soon there was a labor shortage.

Women in the Workplace

Before World War II, most middle- and upper-class women did not work. They were expected to stay home and take care of their families. In minority and lower-class families, money was scarce. The women often had jobs outside the home, but the work was hard and paid little.

The labor shortage World War II created caused many more American women to take a job outside of their homes. Before the war, only 25 percent of American workers were women. By 1945 the number was more than 33 percent.

Women took on many jobs traditionally done by men. Approximately 3 million women worked in war factories as welders, riveters, and electricians. American women built airplanes, ships, and other materials throughout the war.

When the war was over, most women went back to being homemakers. But they had shown they could

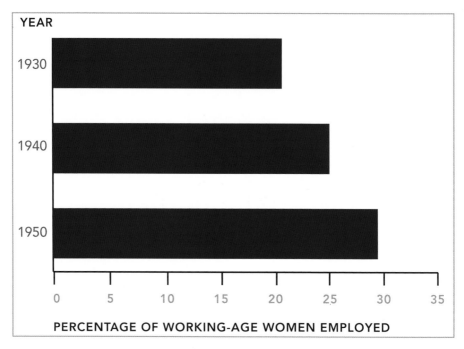

YEAR

1930	
1940	
1950	

0   5   10   15   20   25   30   35

PERCENTAGE OF WORKING-AGE WOMEN EMPLOYED

Women in the Workforce

Before World War II, if a woman had a job, she usually worked in teaching, nursing, or library science. But wartime changed the workforce. This chart shows how the number of working-age women grew significantly during World War II. After reading this chapter, why do you think women were needed in more industries?

do the same jobs as men. Attitudes about women working were beginning to change. Many women fought to keep their jobs in the factories.

The labor shortage also caused many teenagers to leave high school to join the workforce. The number of teenagers in the workforce during the war rose from approximately 1 million to 3 million. As a result, the school drop-out rate also reached an all-time high.

Work for African Americans

Among those looking for work in urban areas were large numbers of African Americans. The labor shortage gave them better job opportunities. But many African Americans still had trouble finding jobs because of their skin color. They faced racism and discrimination from employers. They were usually the last hired and the first fired.

President Roosevelt issued an executive order banning discrimination in government jobs and defense industries. The order was a step in the right direction, but it was not effective. Minorities still faced trouble in their jobs.

The demand for workers during World War II brought about changes in the American workforce. These changes continued even after the war was over.

More and more people, including women, were moving away from rural areas to find work in defense plants located in the cities.

Women took on more demanding jobs. And minorities began seeking equal treatment in the workplace.

Population Shifts

The war brought other changes too. Many people moved to the city to be closer to the factories.

The population began to shift from rural to urban. This population shift also moved many people west. It was a time of development for the western United States.

FURTHER EVIDENCE

There is quite a bit of information about work during World War II in Chapter Two. It also covers women in the workplace. What is one of the main points of this chapter? What key evidence supports this point? Visit the website below to learn more about women working during World War II. Find a quote from the website that supports the chapter's main point. How does the quote support the author's main point? Does it make a new point? Write a few sentences explaining how the quote you found relates to this chapter.

American Women Working
www.mycorelibrary.com/world-war-ii

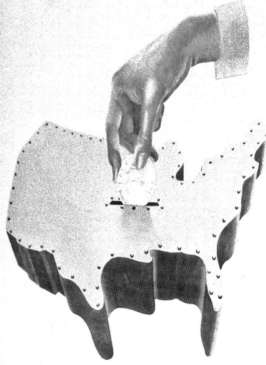

CHAPTER THREE

KEEPING THE HOME FIRES BURNING

While US soldiers were fighting overseas, their families were doing their part at home. They invested in the war by buying war savings bonds. These bonds helped the government raise money. This money was used to pay soldiers and make war materials. It was also a way for Americans to earn interest on their savings. When war bonds matured, buyers could expect to get their money

Americans did everything they could to help the war effort, including buying war bonds.

Kids did their part to help the war effort by collecting scrap metal to be used for war materials.

back plus interest. People could support the war and save money at the same time. War stamps were also introduced during World War II. Those who could afford it bought stamps to fill war bond booklets. Each completed book could be traded in for a war bond.

Doing whatever people could to help the war effort became a way of life. People donated items they did not want or need. Old tires, tin cans, and old farm tools were collected regularly. The items were recycled for use in guns, bullets, and other war materials. Housewives saved their cooking fats for making explosives.

Food and Rationing

American families also had to make sacrifices during the war. The government created a program in 1942 that set limits on the amount of gas, food, and clothing people could buy. There were 20 items that could only be bought with

PERSPECTIVES

Japanese Americans

Two months after the attack on Pearl Harbor, President Roosevelt signed Executive Order 9066 into law. This forced more than 110,000 Japanese people to move to relocation camps. The camps were made up of buildings surrounded by fences and armed guards. The majority of the Japanese who lived there were American citizens. The Japanese were forced to leave their homes and their jobs. Roosevelt and others believed the law was necessary to protect the United States. However, none of the Japanese Americans who were forced to leave their homes were ever proven to be disloyal.

government-issued stamps. The stamps were similar to coupons. Rationed items included sugar, meat, butter, fruit, shoes, clothing, tires, gas, and oil. People were only allowed to buy rationed items if they had the right stamp.

Many Americans started home gardens, nicknamed victory gardens. People grew vegetables, fruits, and herbs. These gardens meant families had to buy less with their food stamps. By 1943 there were more than 2 million victory gardens. The gardens produced at least one-third of the vegetables eaten by Americans.

Ration Books

Rationing was a way to make sure everyone had a fair share of the food and supplies available. Eight thousand ration groups were set up to oversee this process. Stamps were only good for a certain amount of time. Some stamps provided an equal share of a product to everyone. Other stamps worked like points that could be used to buy items such as meat or diary. Still other stamps were given based on need.

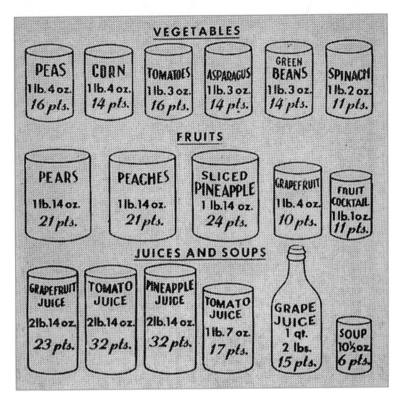

Rationing Point System

This illustration helps explain the rationing point system in 1943. Each person within a household received 48 points per month for canned, dried, and frozen foods. A person could not purchase more of these goods once their points were gone. If you had 48 points to use on food, how would you spend your points for the month? How does this illustration help give you a better understanding of the limited resources and food during World War II?

Clothing

New clothes were rare because of rationing during World War II. Many of the materials used in shoes and clothing were now used in making war supplies.

Silk was used to make parachutes. Metal for zippers and buttons was harder to find. Hemlines went up and sleeves got shorter because fabric was being rationed. The only way to get new shoes was to have the money and the right ration stamp.

Most Americans made these sacrifices because they believed in their cause. They were willing to do their part to protect their home and their freedoms. Americans believed their sacrifices were helping other countries too.

Many children did not have money or ration coupons for new clothes or shoes. Sometimes they had to wear hand-me-downs or clothes they did not like. This excerpt about life during World War II describes what one girl thought of the fashion:

> I took note the first day [of school] that things were going to be pretty different . . . I had a problem. First of all, I didn't have shoes. We got only two shoe-ration coupons a year, and I had spent mine on the farm on cowboy boots and ice skates and I promised I wouldn't complain about not having shoes. My brother donated his black high-top basketball shoes, and I had to wear them. They looked really great along with my chickenfeed-sack dresses (which were common on the farm) and my country braids and no makeup. I realized right away at school that I was not going to be a social success.
>
> Source: Mark Jonathan Harris, Franklin Mitchell, and Steven Schechter. The Homefront: America During World War II. New York: Putnam, 1984. 34.

Back It Up

The author of this passage is using evidence to support a point. Write a paragraph describing the point the author is making. Then write down two or three pieces of evidence the author uses to make the point.

CHAPTER FOUR

SCHOOL AND PLAY

World War II touched the life of each American. Everyone understood the importance of civil defense and a united effort. It included everything from collecting scrap metals to serving as air-raid wardens or plane spotters. Winning the war was going to take the efforts of the entire country, including children.

Students often took part in scrap drives at their schools.

Windows were covered with blankets during blackout drills.

Volunteering

Everyone was encouraged to find ways to volunteer. For most children, school went on as usual. Much of children's volunteer work took place at school. Students collected scrap metal, old rubber, cooking fats, and old newspapers. These were used for making bullets and other war materials. And at least part of each school day was spent discussing war news or other patriotic topics. Geography lessons often focused on the location of the fighting.

Outside of school, children often volunteered in other ways. Boys often helped during blackout drills. A blackout meant all lights in a town were turned off, including car headlights. Lights were also blocked using blankets. The drills were practice in case an enemy plane was spotted nearby. Then the whole town would be blacked out to avoid becoming a bomb target.

Children also helped to earn money for their families. In the South, children could help pick cotton. They earned one penny for each pound of

Youth Volunteers

The Boy Scouts of America played an important role during World War II. They sold war bonds and hosted scrap drives. Boy Scouts also collected items to send to US soldiers and those affected by the war in Europe. The Girl Scouts did their part too. They collected silk stockings needed to make parachutes. Girl Scouts made sweaters, socks, and blankets for US troops. They also babysat for women working in the defense plants. Some of the older girls helped in hospitals.

Kids enjoyed playing outside on the playground equipment.

cotton. The money earned was used to help pay for clothes and other necessary items.

Wartime Toys

Throughout the war, toys were usually made of wood, paper, or certain kinds of cloth. These items weren't needed for war supplies. For lucky children, a birthday or Christmas present meant a paper doll, a wooden toy, or a puzzle. Children also had fun in the neighborhood. They played games such as hopscotch, four square, marbles, jump rope, and hide-and-seek. On rainy days, it was fun to play checkers while listening to the radio.

School and playtime activities went on as usual during the war. But the thought of the war was never far from anyone's mind. People worried there might be another attack on US soil. In addition, almost everyone had a family member serving in the military. The worries of the war weighed on everyone.

PERSPECTIVES
Freedom for All?

For most Americans, the war was about freedom for all people. But not all Americans enjoyed the same freedoms. Many African-American families moved west to find work during the war. They hoped to leave a segregated, or separated, society behind them. But they found many of the same problems in the West. There were separate restrooms, water fountains, entrances, and schools. Some Americans began to question this treatment. The United States was fighting a war against such practices overseas. Americans argued that if it was wrong for Hitler to discriminate against Jewish people, it was wrong for Americans to discriminate against African Americans.

CHAPTER FIVE

THAT'S ENTERTAINMENT!

During World War II, American homes had no cell phones or computers. Few homes had televisions. Most families had a radio, but not everyone had a telephone. Newspapers and radio provided most of the news about the war. Every evening Americans tuned in their radios to hear famous news anchors Walter Winchell or Edward R. Murrow report the news. For the first six

Many families listened to radio shows in the evenings, including Bob Hope's show.

Almost 60 million people went to the movies each week between 1942 and 1946.

months of US involvement in the war, it was often bad. But soon, US-made war materials began rolling off the production lines. More US soldiers finished their training and joined the battle.

The radio also provided entertainment for families. It was a way to forget about the war for a few minutes. Music and comedy shows such as the *Pepsodent Program* with actor Bob Hope were popular. There were dramatic programs such as the *Lux Radio Theatre*. And big band leaders such as Tommy Dorsey and Glenn Miller played the music of the day for eager listeners.

Movies

Another escape from the sacrifices of wartime was a trip to the movies. During the war years, Hollywood did its part to encourage support for the war and provide entertainment. Movie attendance reached its peak during these years.

The average cost of a movie ticket was approximately 27 cents. This bought you a newsreel, a cartoon, and the main feature. The newsreels were

Hollywood Goes to War

Throughout World War II, Hollywood made movies and documentaries in support of the war. Movies, newsreels, and even cartoons all portrayed the enemy as weak. Hollywood filmmaker Frank Capra produced a series of seven documentaries from 1943 to 1945. The *Why We Fight* series emphasized the importance of victory for the Allies. It also encouraged support for the war. The objective of Hollywood propaganda was to help build unity and commitment among Americans. Some historians might argue that this one-sided view of the war was unfair. However, most US leaders felt Hollywood's support was vital to the war effort.

Many stars of the 1940s, including the Andrews Sisters, traveled with the United Service Organization (USO) anywhere there were Allied servicemen.

approximately ten minutes long and provided pictures from the war. Cartoons were funny and often portrayed the enemy as clumsy. The feature films created famous movie stars. These stars also helped out with war efforts.

Movie Stars and the USO

The movie stars of the war years did much more than make movies. They all did their best to keep the country's morale high. They entertained troops, sold war bonds, and provided labor and entertainment in military clubs all across the country.

The United Service Organization (USO) sponsored many of these clubs. The USO was first established in 1941. This was before the United States entered the war. The USO's mission was to boost troop morale and provide entertainment. The USO built canteens, or clubs, for soldiers. Any soldier could go in for a free meal and be entertained by Hollywood stars.

Americans celebrate the end of World War II, which brought about great changes for the country.

The USO also took their show on the road. They put on shows in cities across the country that included musical numbers, dances, skits, and comedy routines.

The End of the War

By September 1945, World War II was over. VE (Victory in Europe) Day was declared May 8, 1945, with the surrender of Germany. A few months later, Japan also surrendered. September 2, 1945, was declared VJ (Victory in Japan) Day.

The war changed the United States. The nation now led the world in producing weapons, food, and supplies. US resourcefulness had helped shorten the war. The successes and confidence gained because of the war led to an economic boom in the years that followed.

EXPLORE ONLINE

The website below has even more information about World War II. As you know, every source is different. Reread Chapter Five of this book. What are the similarities between Chapter Five and the information you found on the website? Are there any differences? How do the two sources present information differently?

The History of the USO
www.mycorelibrary.com/world-war-ii

Sally lives with her mother and two brothers near Saint Louis, Missouri. Sally's dad is away serving in the US Navy. Because Sally's mom is working to help the war effort, Sally has to help at home.

6:00 a.m.
Sally wakes up and gets dressed for school. She wakes her younger brothers and helps them get ready for school.

7:00 a.m.
Sally makes lunches for the whole family while her mother cooks breakfast. Then her mother leaves to catch the bus for her job at the factory. Sally cleans the kitchen before she and the boys leave for school.

8:30 a.m.
Sally and her brothers walk to school. They each take two pennies to buy stamps for a savings booklet.

3:30 p.m.
Sally and her brothers walk home from school. At home Sally slices an apple three ways and takes out three cookies for a snack.

4:00 p.m.

Sally finishes her homework and goes out to tend the victory garden. The boys pull weeds while Sally picks three squash that have ripened. Then she feeds the chickens and collects the eggs.

5:30 p.m.

Sally's mother will be home soon. Sally starts dinner. She slices the squash and puts them in a pot with a small amount of water, sugar, butter, salt, pepper, and chopped onion. She is careful not to waste the butter or sugar because those items are rationed.

7:30 p.m.

Sally walks to her friend Laura's house. Laura's mother is the Girl Scout leader. Tonight they are going to roll bandages and make care packages for the soldiers.

9:00 p.m.

Sally arrives home in time to listen to the *Kraft Music Hall* radio program with her mother for the rest of the evening.

Dig Deeper

After reading this book, what questions do you still have about World War II? Do you want to learn more about everyday life? Write down one or two questions that can guide you in doing research. With an adult's help, find a few reliable sources about this time period that can help answer your questions. Write a few sentences about how you did your research and what you learned from it.

Another View

This book has a lot of information about daily life during World War II. As you know, every source is different. Ask a librarian or another adult to help you find another source about World War II. Write a short essay comparing and contrasting the new source's point of view with that of this book. What is the point of view of each author? How are they similar and why? How are they different and why?

Surprise Me

Chapter Two discusses women in the workforce. After reading this book, what two or three facts about women in the workforce did you find most surprising? Write a few sentences about each fact. Why did you find them surprising?

Tell the Tale

Chapter Four discusses air-raid drills. Write 200 words that tell the story of living through a drill. Describe the sights and sounds you see. What are you supposed to do during the drill? Be sure to set the scene, develop a sequence of events, and offer a conclusion.

GLOSSARY

ammunition
bullets, bombs, or anything that can be fired from a gun or that can explode

canteens
places where supplies or refreshments are sold or provided

civil defense
actions of civilians to defend people and property in a time of war

dictator
a ruler with complete power who often governs in a cruel or unfair way

discrimination
to treat some people better than others for an unfair reason, such as skin color

interest
a charge for borrowed money that is generally a percentage of the amount borrowed

morale
the state of mind of a person or group

ration
to give out or make available in fixed amounts or portions

riveters
people who join two or more metal plates, pieces, or objects using metal bolts

spotters
people whose civil defense responsibility was to look out for enemy aircraft

LEARN MORE

Books

Adams, Simon. *World War II*. New York: DK Publishing, 2010.

Atwood, Kathryn J. *Women Heroes of World War II: 26 Stories of Espionage, Sabotage, Resistance, and Rescue*. Chicago: Chicago Review Press, 2011.

Hamen, Susan E. *Pearl Harbor*. Minneapolis: Abdo Publishing, 2009.

Websites

To learn more about Daily Life in US History, visit **booklinks.abdopublishing.com.** These links are routinely monitored and updated to provide the most current information available.

Visit **www.mycorelibrary.com** for free additional tools for teachers and students.

INDEX

ABOUT THE AUTHOR

Wendy H. Lanier is a former teacher who writes and speaks for children and adults. Recently, she also became a speech language pathologist. She and her husband of 26 years have three dogs, two daughters, and two granddaughters.